LOCAL RED BOOK

FAREHAM GOSPORT

PORTCHESTER · STUBBINGTON

CONTENTS

Redbooks showing the way

Every effort has been made to verify the accuracy of information in this book but the publishers cannot accept responsibility for expense or loss caused by an error or omission.

Information that will be of assistance to the user of the maps will be welcomed.

The representation on these maps of a road, track or path is no evidence of the existence of a right of way.

Street plans prepared and published by ESTATE PUBLICATIONS, Bridewell House, TENTERDEN, KENT. The Publishers acknowledge the co-operation of the local authorities of towns represented in this atlas.

Ordnance Survey® This product includes mapping data licensed from Ordnance Survey® with the permission of the Controller of Her Majesty's Stationery Office.

© Crown Copyright   070-14/06-04   All rights reserved
© Estate Publications   ISBN 1 84192 349 4   Licence Number 100019031

www.ESTATE-PUBLICATIONS.co.uk

Legend

- Minor Road
- Pedestrianized / Restricted Access
- Track
- Built Up Area
- Footpath
- Stream
- River
- Lock — Canal
- Railway / Station
- ● Post Office
- P   P+ — Car Park / Park & Ride
- C Public Convenience
- ✚ Place of Worship
- → One-way Street
- i Tourist Information Centre
- 🔺8 🔺8 Adjoining Pages
- Area Depicting Enlarged Centre
- Emergency Services
- Industrial Buildings
- Leisure Buildings
- Education Buildings
- Hotels etc.
- Retail Buildings
- General Buildings
- Woodland
- Orchard
- Recreational / Parkland
- Cemetery

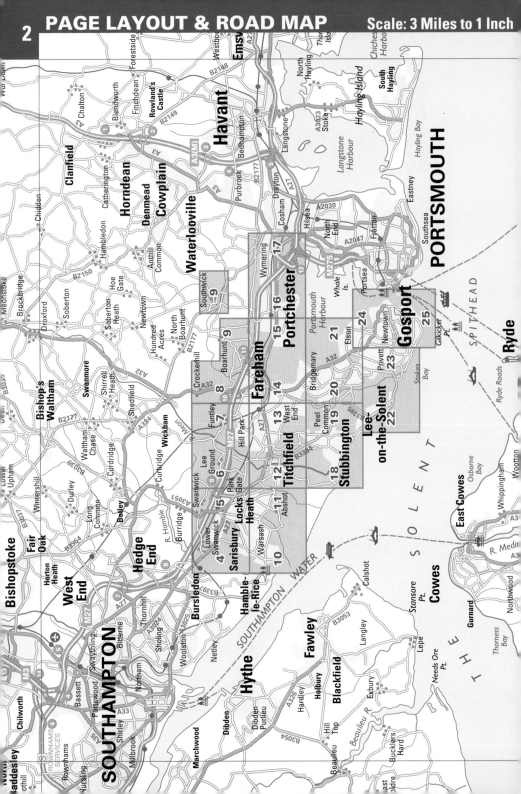

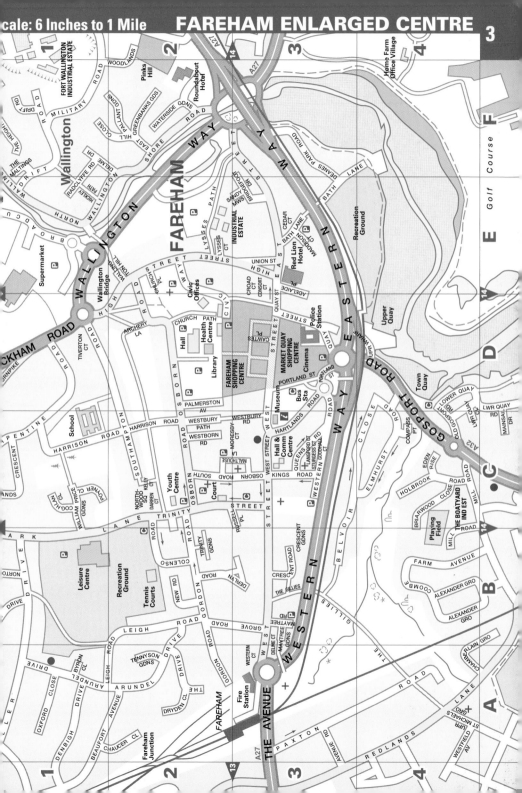

A **B** **C** **D**

1

2

3

4

5

6

Flagpond Copse

Stonyfield Copse

Landfill Site

Playing Field

Superstore

WHITELEY VILLAGE DESIGNER OUTLET

Hall

Whiteley Farm Roundabout

Round Coppice

Hotel

ROOKERY AV

Whiteley Way Roundabout

SOLENT BUSINESS PARK

Lee Ground Coppice

Club House

PEGHAM INDUSTRIAL PARK

LAVEYS LANE

Pegham Coppice

Hazel Coppice

Golf Course

Gulley Coppice

MEADOWS

LAVEYS LA

SPRINGLES LANE

IRONMILL LANE

INDUSTRIAL ESTATE

CONCORDE

SEGENSWORTH NORTH INDUSTRIAL ESTATE

WITHERBED WAY

LADY BETTY DRIVE

Lee Ground

Berry Coppice

Moorshill Farm

River Meon

M27

NORTH EAST INDUSTRIAL ESTATE

BRUNEL

WITHERBED

Caravan Site

FUNTLEY ROAD

SEGENSWORTH EAST INDUSTRIAL ESTATE

BARNES WALLIS

Park Farm

Household Waste Recycling Centre

CARTWRIGHT ROAD

Ashlyn Farm

SEGENSWORTH ROAD

Offices

ST LEONARDS CL

Titchfield Park

Works

SEGENSWORTH ROAD

MILL LANE

School

FUNTLEY ROAD

A **B** **C** **D**

12

E F G H

Mushes Copse

Works
Cemy

NORTH PARK BUSINESS CENTRE

North Park Farm

MAYLES CORNER

Ravenswood House

MAYLES LANE

HORSESHOE

KNOWLE

PIPISTRELLE WK

VICTORIA MEWS

KNOWLE AV

KNOWLE

KNOWLE AV

Knowle Village

SAXE CT

CHARITY

DEAN VILLAS

TITCHFIELD

Great Funtley Farm

MAYLES LANE

RIVER

TITCHFIELD LANE

LEY RD

FUNTLEY LANE

ROEBUCK AV

STAG AV

DEER LEAP

ROEBUCK

WAY

HONEY LANE

Football Grnd

FUNTLEY ROAD

FUNTLEY LA

FUNTLEY

Funtley

Great Beamond Coppice

LAKESIDE

THE WATERS

FUNTLEY ROAD

FUNTLEY HILL

Kneller Court

Hookhouse Coppice

Little Beamond Coppice

Fareham Tunnel

Fareham Lane

Fareham Common

KNELLER COURT

LECHLADE GDNS

THE COPSE

THE GLADE

KINGSTON GDNS

WALTON

RUNNYMEDE

THAMES DRIVE

HENLEY

RED

MARLOW CL

SUNBURY

BARN

HOLLY WY LODGE

GREEN HOLLOW

HIGHLANDS

ROAD

THE CEDARS

POTTERS AV

GREEN WOOD

KILN

BURNHAM WOOD

FAREHAM

PARK CT

WHINCHAT CL

HILLSON

THORNI

HILL PARK RD

GREENDALE CL

THE GREENDALE

WINNINGTON

HILL PARK

Orch Lea Junior School

BEAUMONT RISE

HILL BROW

KENNEDY AV

HIGH MEAD

HIGH WK

GRN WK

WOODHALL WY

MARY ROSE CL

HOYLEACRE

MILLER

CRAWFORD

WAKEFIELD AV

ODELL CL

LONGSTAFF FARM

SAVILLE GDNS

TENSING CL

IRVINE CL

BURNHAM WOOD

Hill Park

PARK FARM AV

ATKINS PL

PARK FARM CL

HAYES CL

PENNINGTON

BEAUMONT

BEAUMONT RISE

ROAD

FROSTHOLE

HILL PARK

COPPICE

WYNTON WAY

TEWKESBURY AV

IRON MILL CLOSE

School

P

LEE OAK GDNS

NASHE WAY

COPPICE

ROAD

HIGH

HEATHER GDNS

CRAVEN CT

STOW

GUDGE

BIFFORD

13

INVERNESS CL

RANNOCH CT

DUNDEE

BARTLETT

FROSTHOLE CL

STIRLING

ANGUS CL

BALMORAL

ABERDEEN

CRES

BRAEMAR

AVENUE

FROSTHOLE CRES

ARGYLE CRES

HILLARY CL

BEAUFORT AVENUE

MAYLINGS

SOMERVELL DRIVE

MORSHEAD

School

NORTON

MALLORY

SOMERVELL

CRESCENT

BRUCE CL

DRIVE

MILLER

BENTLEY CL

KELLER

1

2

3

4

5

6

Cr

Knowle

Up

Crecreation ground

munity centre

Hill Park RD

E F G H

A   **B**   **C**   **D**

1

Blakes Copse

A32

WICKHAM

Heytesbury Farm

Saw Mill

Carpenters Copse

Homerhill Copse

Crockerhill

Pigeonhous Copse

FOREST

2

ROAD

KNOWLE

CHALK LA

ROAD

ALBANY BUSINESS CENTRE

Albany Farm

7

Charity Farm

ROAD

3

WICKHAM

River

Wallington

Whitedell Farm

LANE

School

4

Dean Farm

POOK

WHITEDELL

7

M27 JUNCTION 10

North Fareham

POOK

LANE

NINE SPURLINGS

ELMS LAN

mon **5**

LANE

North Fareham Farm

Spurlings Farm

M27

SPURLINGS IND EST

Down Barn Farm

ROAD

BOARHUNT ROAD

6

POTTERS AV

GREEN WOOD CL

WEST DOWNS CL

KILN

NORTH HILL

WICKHAM

SWALLOW FIELD

FURZEHALL

FURZE

AVENUE

HAREBELL

THE MEADOWS

FOXGLOVES

WAY

STANDARD

FAREHAM INDUSTRIAL PARK

WALLINGTON

North Wallington

FAREHAM HEIGHTS

WAY

Uplands

ROAD

KILN

BURNHAM WOOD

THE MALLARDS

LANE OLD

BURNHAM WOOD

TENSING CL

MALLC

NE

Cemetery

FURZEHALL GDNS

FILNHANOW GDNS

PENNANT PK

STANDARD

NORTH

BROADCUT

BRIDGE INDUSTRIAL ESTATE

THE HEIGHTS

RIVERSIDE AV

North Wallington

School

CRESCENT

CL NORTON

BRUCE CL

DRIVE NORTON

PARK

KILN ACRE

THE POTTERIES

ST SEBASTIAN CRES

ST CHRISTOPHER AV

ST THOMAS ST

HOSP

PENNANT PK

STANDARD

WALLINGTON

DR

LIFT RD

FORT WALLINGTON

SOMERVELL DR

MILLER DRIVE

DRIVE

MEAD

SERPENTINE RD

UPLANDS CRES

SERPENT

TURNPIKE

ROAD

A32

TURNPIKE

BKH

Supermarket

ADCUT

A27

A   **B**   **C**   **D**

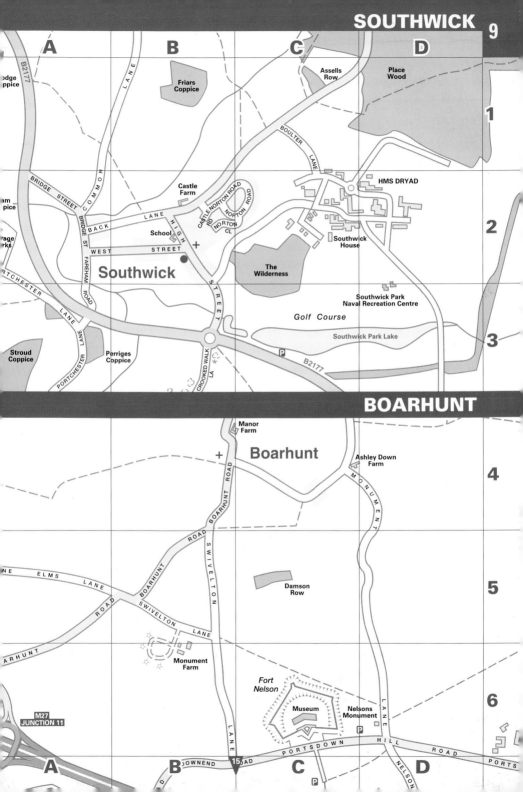

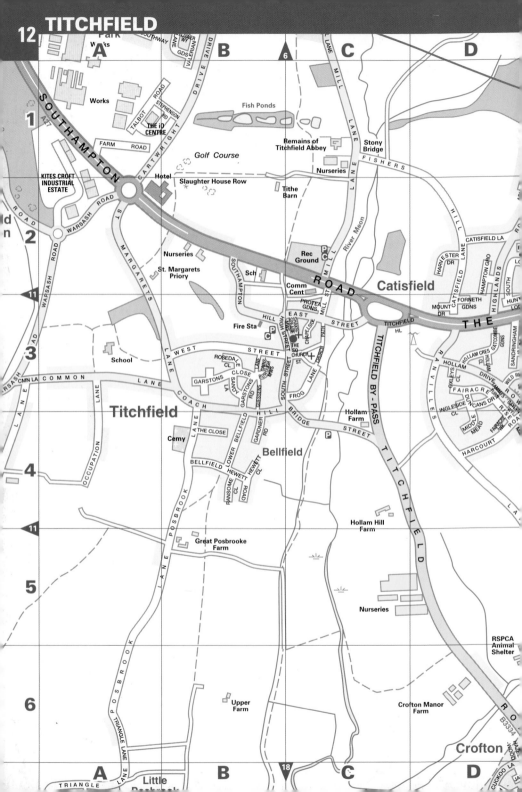

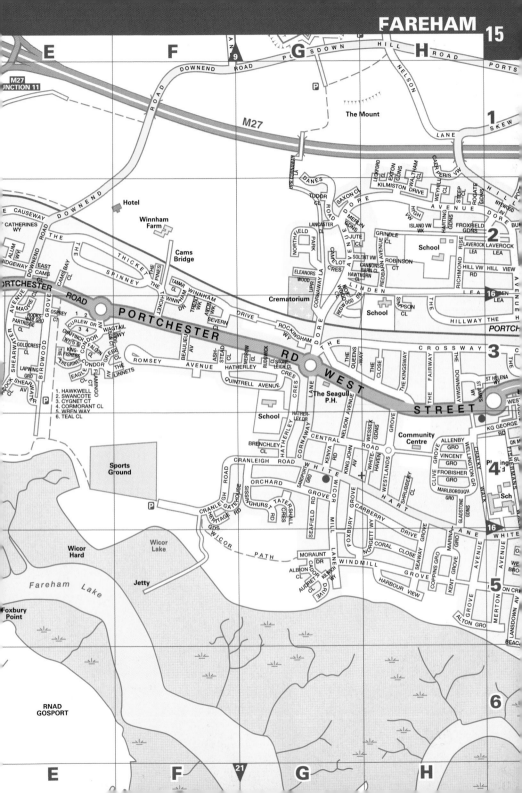

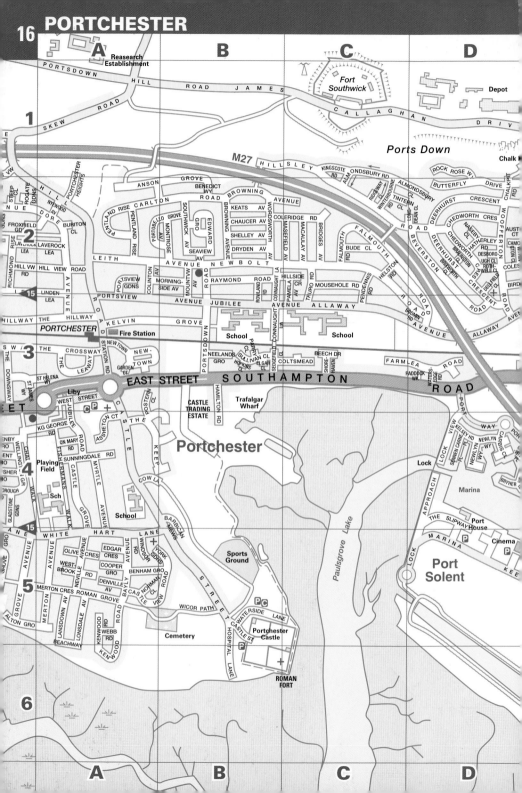

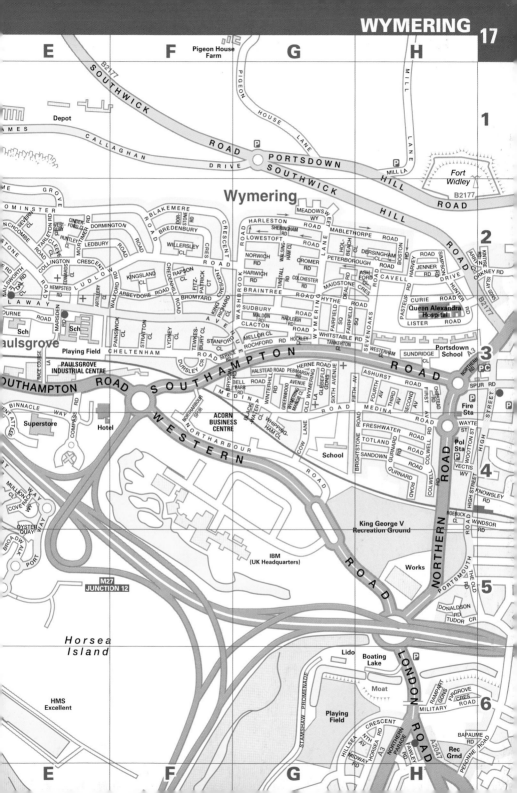

A   B   C   C D'ton

Little Posbrook

Triangle

Lower Posbrook Farm

Thatchers Coppice

Churchers Row

Meon

Stubbington

Meon View Farm

River Meon

Titchfield Haven

Visitor Centre

Hill Head Sailing Club

Hillhead Harbour

Hill Head

Osborne View Hotel

THE SOLENT

Salterns Par

A   B   C   D

1
2
3
4
5
6

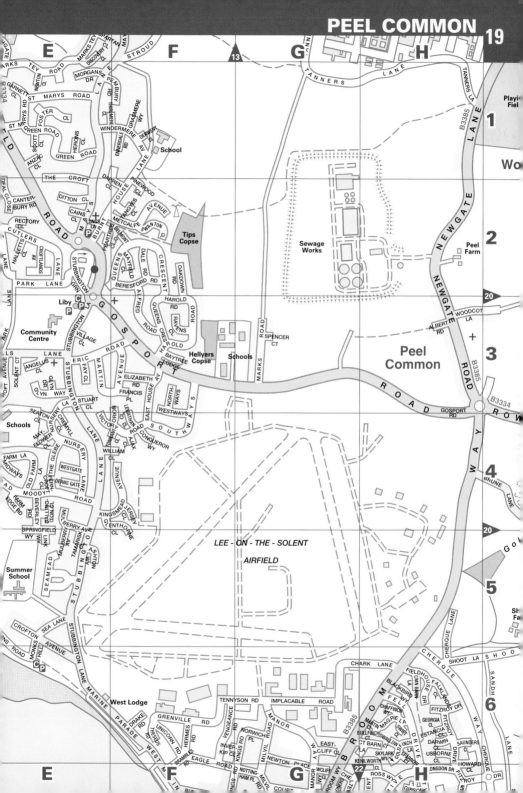

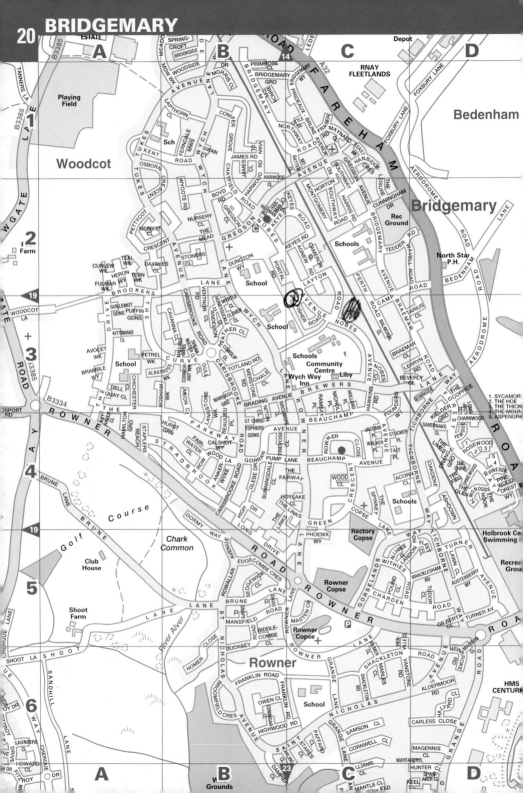

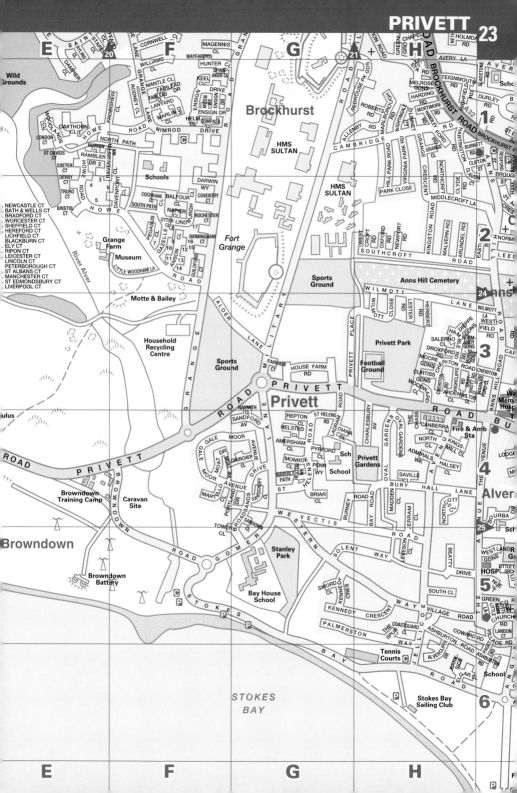

STREET

5   6   7   8

F

E

D

C

B

A

Fort Blockhouse

Marina

Floating Dock

HMS Submarine Alliance

RN Submarine Museum

Haslar Bridge

FORT BLOCKHOUSE

Joint Services Adventurous Sail Training Centre

DEFENCE EVALUATION & RESEARCH ESTABLISHMENT

ROYAL HOSPITAL

Cemetery Disused

HM Detention Centre

Club Ho

Fort Monckton

Gilkicker Point

Sand

Spit

SEA WALL

HASLAR

Haslar Lake

RAMPART RW

MARINERS WY

DOLMAN RD

THORN BRAKE RD

HILTON CL

HORNET RD

OLD ROAD

WORKHOUSE LAKE

MAYFIELD ROAD

Alver Bridge

SUNBEAM

DOLPHIN CRES

CROSS-LAND CL

Gosport Park

The Dell

Stoke Lake

Clayhall

Haslar Royal Naval Cemetery

DOLPHIN WAY

HASLAR ROAD

WATERLOO RD

BEVOL

MAIN ROAD

GILKICKER

FORCE RD

WILBER WORTH

HABEL

CONSTABLE DR

ST FRANCIS RD

REGAN

THE AV

SPITHEAD AV

LIND RD

WATERLOO RD

LONG DR

LENNOX

Recreation Ground

Moat

Fort Gilkicker

Golf Course

CRANBOURNE RD

AYLESBURY

SINGTON RD

ESWORTH RD

VER RD

CLEVELAND RD

ST PR ALFRED RD

STONE CL

ST RD

Sch

THE PAD

THE MOUND

FOSTER Gardens

LINDEN

Anglesey Gardens

BEECH GRO

PARK ROAD

LEYLAND

ST VALERIE RD

ALECTO RD

PLEASANT RD

BENTHAM ROAD

Ewer Common

LEWER ROAD

ANGLESEY ROAD

Viaduct

THE HAVEN

ALVARA RD

CLAYHALL ROAD

KENNET CL

BUDDENS RD

ST MARKS RD

ARMIERS RD

Hall

ATKINSON

ANGLESEY ARMS

ELLACHIE RD

ELLACHIE GDNS

ELLACHIE MWS

Anglesey

MONCKTON ROAD

NEPTUNE CL

PEPYS CL

BRAMLEY GDNS

FORT ROAD

Royal Naval Physiological Laboratory

Stokes Bay Angling Club

Alverstoke

BEECH RD

TESTCOMBE ROAD

BRODERICK ROAD

AVENUE

ST MARYS RD

LITTLE ANGLESEY ROAD

RECTORY CL

SOMERVELL CL

SOMERVELL RD

CRESCENT

School

FORT ROAD

School

Rec Grnd

HOSP

WEST END GDNS

DURBA

GREEN RD

CHAD LITTLE CT

MWS

PAGET RD

THE VILLAGE ROAD

GARD RD

BANK-SIDE

23

BEATTY

LANE

SEY

THE AVENUE

DRIVE

CL

ROAD

5   6   7   8

The Index includes some names for which there is insufficient space on the maps. These names are indicated by an * and are followed by the nearest adjoining thoroughfare.

Cardinal Way SO31 11 G1
Carisbrooke Av PO14 18 C3
Carisbrooke Rd PO13 20 B2
Carless Cl PO13 20 D6
Carlton Rd, Fareham PO16 16 A2
Carlton Rd, Gosport PO12 24 C4
Carlton Way PO12 24 C4
Carlyle Rd PO12 24 B3
Carnarvon Rd PO12 24 A4
Carne Pl PO6 16 D4
Caroline Gdns PO15 13 E1
Caroline Pl PO12 24 B3
Carran Walk PO14 13 G4
Carraway PO15 5 H2
Cartwright Dr PO15 12 A2
Caspar John Cl PO14 18 D4
Caspian Cl PO15 5 F2
Castle Gro PO16 16 A4
Castle Rd PO17 9 B2
Castle St PO16 16 A3
Castle Trading Est PO16 16 B3
Castle Vw PO12 21 G5
Castle Vw Rd PO16 16 A5
Catamaran Cl SO31 10 D2
Catisfield La PO15 12 D2
Catisfield Rd PO15 13 E2
Cavanna Cl PO13 20 B3
Cavell Dr PO6 17 H2
Cawtes Pl PO16 3 D3
Cedar Cl PO12 21 F5
Cedar Ct PO16 3 E3
Cedar Way PO14 13 G3
Celandine Av SO31 10 D1
Central Rd PO16 15 G4
Centre Way SO31 5 E6
Chaffinch Way, Fareham PO16 15 E3
Chaffinch Way, Lee-on-the-Solent PO13 19 H6
Chale Cl PO13 20 B3
Chalk La PO17 8 B2
Chalkpit Rd PO6 16 D2
Chalky Walk PO16 15 H4
Challenger Dr PO12 24 C1
Chamberlain Gro PO14 3 A4
Chancel Cl SO31 5 F6
Chandlers Way SO31 5 F3
Chantrell Walk PO15 7 F6
Chantry Rd PO12 21 E6
Chapel Rd SO31 4 D3
Chapel Sq PO12 21 E6
Chapel St PO12 21 H5
Chapelside PO14 12 C3
Charden Rd PO13 20 C5
Charfield Cl PO14 13 F3
Charity Vw PO17 7 G2
Chark La PO13 19 G6
Charlemont Dr PO16 14 D2
Charlesbury Av PO12 23 H4
Charlotte Dr PO12 24 C1
Charlotte Mews PO12 25 A6
Charnwood PO13 20 D4
Chartwell Cl PO14 11 G2
Chatfield Rd PO13 20 B1
Chatham Cl PO12 24 C2
Chatsworth Cl PO15 13 E2
Chaucer Av PO6 16 B2
Chaucer Cl PO16 3 A1
Chedworth Cres PO6 16 D2
Cheltenham Cres PO13 22 B1
Cheltenham Rd PO6 17 F3
Cheriton Rd PO12 23 H3
Cherque La PO13 19 H6
Cherque Way PO13 19 H6
Cherry Cl PO13 22 C2
Cherry Tree Av PO14 13 F3
Cherry Walk SO31 10 A3
Cherrygarth Rd PO15 13 E2
Cheshire Cl PO15 6 B4
Chester Cres PO13 22 D4
Chesterton Pl PO15 5 G1
Chestnut Walk PO12 21 G5
Chestnut Way PO14 11 G2
Cheviot Grn SO31 10 C3
Cheviot Walk PO14 13 G4
Cheyne Way PO13 22 C2
Chichester Cl, Lee-on-the-Solent PO13 20 A3
Chichester Cl, Southampton SO31 4 C6
Chilcomb Cl PO13 22 C2
Chilling La SO31 10 D6
Chiltern Walk PO14 13 G4
Chilworth Gro PO12 24 A3
Chine Cl SO31 5 E5
Chipstead Rd PO6 17 H3
Christie Av PO15 5 H1
Church Cl SO31 5 F6
Church La SO31 4 A1
Church Path, Fareham PO16 3 D2
Church Path, Gosport PO12 24 D4
Church Path, Titchfield PO14 12 C3
Church Pl PO16 3 E2
Church Rd, Gosport PO12 25 A6
Church Rd, Locks Heath SO31 5 F6
Church Rd, Warsash SO31 10 B2
Church St PO14 12 C3
Churcher Cl PO12 23 G4
Churcher Walk*, Churcher Cl PO12 23 G4
Churchill Cl PO14 11 G2
Cinderford Cl PO6 17 E2
Civic Way PO16 3 D2
Clacton Rd PO6 17 G3
Clanwilliam Rd PO13 22 B2
Clare Cl PO14 11 G2
Clarence Rd PO12 24 D3
Clarendon Cres PO14 11 G2
Claudia Ct PO12 23 H1
Clayhall Rd PO12 25 A6
Clee Av PO14 13 F3
Cleeve Cl PO6 17 E2
Clement Attlee Way PO6 17 E3
Cleric Ct PO14 5 H6
Cleveland Dr PO14 13 F3
Cleveland Rd PO12 25 B5
Cliff Rd PO14 18 B4
Clifton Rd PO13 22 C3
Clifton St PO12 23 H1
Clipper Cl SO31 10 C2
Clive Gro PO16 15 H4
Clover Cl, Lee-on-the-Solent PO13 20 B3
Clover Cl, Southampton SO31 10 D1
Clyde Ct*, Clyde Rd PO12 23 H2
Clyde Rd PO12 23 H2
Clydesdale Rd PO15 5 F2
Coach Hill PO14 12 B3
Coal Park La SO31 4 C1
Coastguard Cl PO12 23 H5
Cobden St PO12 24 B3
Cobham Gro PO15 6 B4
Cochrane Cl PO13 23 F2
Cockerell Cl PO15 5 G4
Cockleshell Cl SO31 10 D2
Coghlan Cl PO16 3 C1
Colchester Rd PO6 17 G2
Coldeast Cl SO31 4 D4
Coldeast Way SO31 5 E4
Colenso Rd PO16 3 B2
Coleridge Cl SO31 10 C3
Coleridge Rd PO6 16 B2
Colesbourne Rd PO6 16 D2
Colinton Av PO16 16 A2
Collingsworth Rise SO31 5 F3
Collington Cres PO6 17 E2
Coltsfoot Dr SO31 10 D1
Coltsmead PO6 16 B3
Colwell Rd PO6 17 H4
Commodore Pl PO12 24 D2
Common Barn La PO13 19 H6
Common La, Southwick PO17 9 A2
Common La, Titchfield PO14 12 A3
Compass Cl PO13 23 F1
Compass Point PO16 3 C4
Compass Rd PO6 17 E4
Compton Cl PO13 22 C2
Concorde Cl PO15 5 H4
Concorde Way PO15 6 A4
Condor Av PO16 15 E3
Conference Dr SO31 5 F6
Conifer Gro PO13 20 B1
Coniston Walk PO14 13 G4
Connaught La PO6 16 B3
Connemara Cres SO31 5 F2
Connigar Cl PO13 20 B6
Conqueror Way PO14 19 F4
Conrad Gdns PO15 5 G1
Consort Ct PO16 3 E3
Constable Cl PO12 25 B7
Coombe Farm Av PO16 3 B4
Coombe Rd PO12 24 B1
Coombedale SO31 11 F2
Coome Farm Av PO16 14 A3
Cooper Gro PO16 16 A5
Coppice Way PO15 7 F6
Coppins Gro PO16 15 H5
Copse La PO13 20 C4
Coracle Cl SO31 10 D2
Coral Cl PO16 15 H5
Corfe Cl PO14 18 C4
Coriander Way PO15 6 A1
Cormorant Cl PO16 15 E3
Cormorant Walk PO13 20 B3
Cornaway La PO16 15 G4
Cornfield PO16 8 B5
Cornfield Rd PO13 22 B1
Cornflower Cl SO31 10 D1
Cornwell Cl PO13 20 C6
Coronado Rd PO12 24 B2
Cort Way PO15 7 E5
Corvette Av SO31 11 E2
Cotswold Walk PO14 13 G4
Cottage Gro PO12 24 B3
Cottes Way PO14 18 C4
Cottesway East PO14 18 D4
Coulmere Rd PO12 24 A2
Country Vw PO14 18 D1
County Gdns PO14 13 E3
Course Park Cres PO14 11 H1
Court Barn Cl*, Court Barn La PO13 19 H6
Court Barn La PO13 19 H6
Court Rd PO13 22 B1
Courtenay Cl PO15 5 H6
Coventry Ct PO13 23 F2
Coverack Way PO6 17 E4
Cow La, Fareham PO16 16 A4
Cow La, Portsmouth PO6 17 G4
Coward Rd PO12 23 H5
Cowdray Pk PO14 18 C3
Cowes La SO31 10 C6
Cowslip Cl, Lee-on-the-Solent PO13 20 B3
Cowslip Cl, Southampton SO31 10 D1
Coxdale PO14 11 G2
Crableck La SO31 4 B4
Crabthorne Farm La PO14 18 D3
Cranborne Walk PO14 13 G4
Cranbourne Rd PO12 25 C5
Cranleigh Rd PO16 15 F4
Craven Ct PO15 7 F6
Crawford Dr PO16 7 H6
Credenhill Rd PO6 17 F2
Creek Rd PO12 24 D4
Cremyll Cl PO14 19 E4
Crescent Gdns PO16 3 B3
Crescent Rd, Fareham PO16 3 B3
Crescent Rd, Gosport PO12 25 A6
Crescent Rd, Southampton SO31 11 E1
Crest Cl PO16 14 D2
Crispin Cl SO31 5 G5
Croad Ct PO16 3 E3
Croftlands Av PO14 19 E2
Crofton Av PO13 19 E5
Crofton La PO14 18 D5
Crofton Way SO31 10 A2
Cromarty Cl PO14 18 D2
Cromer Rd PO6 17 G2
Cromhall Cl PO14 13 E3
Crompton Way PO15 5 G4
Crooked Walk La PO17 9 B3
Cross Rd PO13 22 C3
Crossfell Walk PO14 13 G4
Crossland Cl PO12 25 C5
Cuckoo La PO14 18 D1
Culloden Cl PO15 13 G1
Cumber Rd SO31 4 D6
Cunningham Dr, Lee-on-the-Solent PO13 20 C2
Cunningham Dr, Southampton SO31 5 F5
Curie Rd PO6 17 H3
Curlew Dr PO16 15 E3
Curlew Walk PO13 20 A2
Curtiss Gdns PO12 23 H3
Cutlers La PO14 19 E2
Cutter Av SO31 10 D2
Cygnet Ct PO16 15 E3
Cyprus Rd PO14 11 G2

Daisy La, Gosport PO12 24 A4
Daisy La, Southampton SO31 5 G6
Dale Dr PO13 14 B6
Dale Rd PO14 19 F2
Dalewood Rd PO15 13 F2
Dallington Cl PO14 19 E4
Dampier Cl PO13 23 E1
Dandelion Cl PO13 20 B3
Danehurst Pl SO31 11 E1
Danes Rd PO16 15 G2
Darren Cl PO14 19 E1
Darren Ct PO16 3 C2
Dartmouth Cl PO12 24 C1
Darwin Cl PO13 19 H6
Darwin Way PO13 23 F2
Davenport Cl PO13 23 F2
David Newberry Dr PO13 22 C1
Davis Cl PO13 20 B5
Davis Way PO14 14 A5
Dayshes Cl PO13 20 A2
Deacon Rd SO31 11 G1
Deal Cl PO14 19 E2
Deal Rd PO6 17 G3
Dean Villas PO17 7 F2
Deane Gdns PO13 22 C1
Deanes Park Rd PO16 3 F3
Deans Gate PO14 19 E4
Deer Leap PO15 7 F4
Deerhurst Cres PO6 16 D2
Defoe Cl PO15 5 G1
Delft Cl SO31 4 D6
Dell Quay Cl PO13 20 A3
Dellfield Cl PO6 16 D2
Delme Ct PO16 3 A3
Delme Dr PO16 3 F2
Denbigh Dr PO16 3 A1
Dene Cl SO31 4 D5
Denham Cl PO14 18 D3
Denville Av PO16 16 A5
Derby Ct PO13 23 E2
Derlyn Rd PO16 3 B3
Dersingham Cl PO6 17 H2
Derwent Cl PO14 19 F1
Derwent Rd PO13 22 B2
Desborough Cl PO6 16 D2
Devonshire Way PO14 13 E4
Dewar Cl PO15 5 H4
Diana Cl PO12 23 G4
Dibles Rd SO31 10 C2
Dieppe Gdns PO12 23 H3
Dingle Way SO31 5 F5
Discovery Cl PO14 19 E1
Ditton Cl PO14 19 E2
Dock Rd PO12 24 C4
Dolman Rd PO12 25 C5
Dolphin Cres PO12 25 C5
Dolphin Ct, Fareham PO14 18 D1
Dolphin Ct, Lee-on-the-Solent PO13 22 A1
Dolphin Way PO12 25 C7
Dominie Walk PO13 22 C1
Donaldson Rd PO6 17 H5
Donnelly St PO12 24 A3
Dore Av PO16 15 G3
Dormington Rd PO6 17 E2
Dormy Cl SO31 4 C6
Dormy Way PO13 20 B4
Dorrien Rd PO12 24 B2
Dorstone Rd PO6 17 F2
Dove Gdns SO31 5 F4
Dover Cl PO14 18 D2
Downend Rd PO16 15 E2
Downland Cl SO31 5 E5
Downside PO13 20 D3
Drake Cl SO31 5 F5
Drake Rd PO13 19 F6
Drift Rd PO16 3 E1
Droxford Cl PO12 23 H3
Drummond Rd PO15 6 A5
Dryden Av PO6 16 B2
Dryden Cl PO16 3 A2
Dukes Rd PO12 24 A2
Duncan Rd SO31 5 F4
Duncans Dr PO14 12 D3
Duncton Way PO13 20 B2
Dundee Cl PO15 7 G6
Dunkeld Rd PO12 21 F6
Dunstable Walk PO14 13 F4
Durham St PO12 24 A3
Durley Rd PO12 24 A2
Dursley Cres PO6 17 F3

Eagle Cl PO16 15 E3
Eagle Rd PO13 19 F6
Earls Rd PO16 14 A4
East Cams Cl PO16 15 E2
East Hill Cl PO16 3 F2
East House Av PO14 19 F4
East Lodge PO15 13 E2
East St, Fareham PO16 3 E3
East St, Portchester PO16 16 A3
East St, Titchfield PO14 12 C3
Eastbourne Av PO12 21 E5
Eastbrook Cl, Gosport PO12 21 E5
Eastbrook Cl, Southampton SO31 5 F4
Eastcliff Cl PO13 19 G6
Eastcroft Rd PO12 24 A3
Eastern Par PO16 14 B4
Eastern Way PO16 3 D3
Eastfield Av PO14 13 H5
Eden Rise PO16 3 C4
Edenbridge Way SO31 5 E3
Edgar Cres PO16 16 A5
Edgecombe Cres PO13 20 B5
Edney Path SO31 4 C3
Edward Gro PO16 16 B2
Edwards Cl PO6 17 E2
Elder Cl SO31 10 D1
Eleanors Wood PO16 15 G2
Elgar Cl, Gosport PO12 23 H6
Elgar Cl, Portsmouth PO6 16 B3
Elgin Cl PO15 13 G1
Eliza Pl PO12 24 C3
Elizabeth Ct PO14 13 H5
Elizabeth Rd PO14 19 F3
Elkstone Rd PO6 17 E2
Ellachie Gdns PO12 25 B7
Ellachie Mews PO12 25 B7
Ellachie Rd PO12 25 B7
Ellerslie Cl PO14 18 C4
Elm Gro PO12 24 B3
Elmdale Cl SO31 10 C3
Elmhurst Bsns Pk PO12 24 C4
Elmhurst Rd, Fareham PO16 3 C4
Elmhurst Rd, Gosport PO12 24 C4
Elmore Av PO13 22 C3
Elmore Cl PO13 22 C2
Elmore Rd PO13 22 C3
Elms Rd PO16 14 A4
Elsfred Rd PO14 18 C4
Elson La PO12 21 F5
Elson Rd PO12 21 E5
Ely Ct PO13 23 F2
Embsay Rd SO31 4 B1
Emmanuel Cl PO14 11 G1
Empson Walk PO13 22 C1
Endeavour Cl PO12 24 D4

Holly Gro PO16	7 G5
Holly Hill La SO31	4 A5
Holly St PO12	24 C4
Hollybank PO13	22 B2
Hollybrook Gdns SO31	5 F4
Hollywell Dr PO6	16 D4
Holmdale Rd PO12	21 F6
Holmefield Av PO14	13 H5
Holmgrove PO14	5 G6
Home Rule Rd SO31	5 F5
Homer Cl PO13	20 B6
Honey La PO15	7 F4
Honeysuckle Cl, Lee-on-the-Solent PO13	20 B3
Honeysuckle Cl, Southampton SO31	5 F4
Hood Cl SO31	5 F5
Hook La SO31, PO14	11 E4
Hook Park Rd SO31	10 B4
Hopkins Cl PO6	16 B3
Hornby SO31	10 C3
Hornet Cl, Fareham PO15	13 F1
Hornet Cl, Gosport PO12	25 C5
Horsea Rd PO2	17 H6
Horseshoe Cl PO14	11 H1
Horseshoe Lodge SO31	10 D2
Horton Rd PO13	20 C2
Hospital La PO16	16 B5
House Farm Rd PO12	23 G3
Howard Cl PO13	22 C1
Howe Rd PO13	23 E1
Howerts Cl SO31	10 C4
Hoylake Cl PO13	20 B4
Hoylecroft Cl PO15	7 G5
Hudson Cl PO13	23 E1
Humber Cl PO14	18 D2
Hunter Cl PO13	23 F1
Hunter Rd PO6	17 H2
Hunters Lodge PO15	12 D3
Huntingdon Cl PO14	11 G2
Huntley Cl PO6	17 E2
Hunts Pond Rd SO31, PO14	11 H1
Hurst Cl PO14	18 C4
Hurst Grn PO13	20 B4
Huxley Cl SO31	11 G1
Hyssop Cl PO15	5 H2
Hythe Rd PO6	17 G3
Ibsen Cl PO15	5 G1
Ilex Cres SO31	5 E6
Illustrious Rd PO14	18 D4
Implacable Rd PO13	19 G6
Ingledene Cl PO12	24 B4
Ingleside Cl PO14	12 D4
Inverkip Cl PO13	19 F6
Inverness Av PO15	7 G6
Inverness Rd PO12	24 A3
Invisible Rd PO14	18 D4
Iron Mill Cl PO15	7 F6
Ironbridge Cres SO31	5 E3
Ironmill La PO15	6 D4
Irvine Cl PO16	7 H6
Island View Walk PO16	15 H2
Jacaranda Cl PO15	6 A6
Jacomb Pl PO13	20 C4
Jamaica Pl PO12	24 C4
Jamaica Rd PO12	24 D3
James Callaghan Dr PO17	16 B1
James Cl PO13	20 B1
James Grieve Av SO31	11 F1
James Rd PO12	20 B1
Jarvis Flds SO31	4 A1
Jasmine Ct PO15	6 A1
Jasmine Walk PO14	13 G3
Jason Way PO12	21 E5
Java Dr PO15	5 G2
Jay Cl PO14	18 D1
Jellicoe Av PO12	23 H6
Jenner Rd PO6	17 H2
Jerram Cl PO12	23 H5
Jersey Cl PO14	19 F4
Jervis Dr PO12	24 B3
Jesmond Gro SO31	11 F2
Jessie Rd PO12	24 A4
John Bunyan Cl PO15	5 G1
Johns Rd PO16	14 A4
Johnson Vw PO15	6 A3
Jonathan Rd PO15	13 F2
Joseph St PO12	24 C4
Jubilee Av PO6	16 B3
Jubilee Cl PO14	13 H4
Jubilee Rd, Fareham PO16	16 A3
Jubilee Rd, Gosport PO12	24 B3
Julie Av PO15	13 G2
Jumar Cl SO31	10 B4
Justin Cl PO14	13 G3
Jute Cl PO16	15 G2
Jutland Cl PO15	5 G2
Kealy Rd PO12	24 B2
Keast Walk PO13	20 C1
Keats Av PO6	16 B2
Keel Cl PO13	23 F1
Keith Cl PO12	24 B2
Kelly Ct PO16	3 C2
Kelsey Cl PO14	11 F2
Kelsey Head PO6	16 D4
Kelvin Gro PO16	16 A3
Kenilworth Cl PO13	19 G6
Kennedy Av PO15	7 F6
Kennedy Cres PO12	23 G5
Kennet Cl PO12	25 B6
Kensington Ct PO12	24 C1
Kensington Gdns PO14	11 G1
Kensington Rd PO12	25 C5
Kent Gro PO16	15 H5
Kent Rd PO13	20 A1
Kenwood Rd PO16	16 A5
Kenya Rd PO16	15 G4
Kestrel Cl PO14	18 D1
Keyes Cl PO13	20 C2
Keyes Rd PO13	20 B2
Keyhaven Cl PO13	20 A4
Kielder Gro PO13	20 D4
Kilmiston Dr PO16	15 H2
Kiln Acre PO16	8 B6
Kiln Rd PO16	7 G5
Kilwich Way PO16	15 G5
Kimpton Cl PO13	22 C1
King George Rd PO16	16 A4
King John Av PO16	15 G4
King Richard Cl PO6	17 F3
King St PO12	24 D3
Kingcup Av SO31	10 D1
Kingdom Cl PO15	5 H4
Kingfisher Copse SO31	5 F6
Kingfishers PO16	15 E3
Kings Rd, Fareham PO16	3 C3
Kings Rd, Gosport PO12	24 B4
Kings Rd, Lee-on-the-Solent PO13	22 A1
Kingscote Rd PO6	16 C1
Kingsland Cl PO6	17 F2
Kingsley Rd PO12	21 E6
Kingsmead Av PO14	19 E4
Kingsmill Cl PO12	23 H4
Kingston Gdns PO15	7 F5
Kingston Rd PO12	23 H4
Kites Croft PO14	11 H2
Kites Croft Ind Est PO14	12 A1
Kittiwake Cl PO13	20 A3
Kneller Ct PO16	7 H5
Knights Bank Rd PO14	18 B4
Knights Cl SO31	10 D2
Knottgrass Rd SO31	10 D1
Knowle Av PO17	7 F2
Knowle Rd PO17	7 G2
Kyak Cl SO31	10 D2
Kynon Cl PO14	21 H5
Laburnum Rd PO16	14 A4
Ladram Rd PO12	23 G4
Lady Betty Dr PO15	6 A4
Lakeside, Fareham PO17	7 G4
Lakeside, Lee-on-the-Solent PO13	22 C3
Lambourn Cl PO14	13 F3
Lambourne Dr SO31	5 F6
Lancaster Cl, Fareham PO16	15 G2
Lancaster Cl, Lee-on-the-Solent PO13	22 D3
Landon Ct PO12	25 A6
Landon Rd PO13	20 C5
Lands End Rd SO31	4 A2
Lanes End PO14	18 D3
Langford Ct PO16	3 C3
Langstone Walk, Fareham PO14	13 E3
Langstone Walk, Lee-on-the-Solent PO13	20 B4
Lansdown Av PO16	16 A5
Lanyard Dr PO13	23 F1
Lapthorn Cl PO13	20 B1
Lapwing Cl PO12	24 B3
Lapwing Gro PO16	15 E3
Larch Cl PO13	22 C2
Larchdale Cl SO31	10 C3
Larches Gdns PO15	13 E2
Larkspur Cl SO31	10 D1
Laser Cl SO31	10 D2
Lasham Walk PO14	13 F4
Launceston Cl PO12	24 C1
Laurel Cl, Gosport PO12	24 C1
Laurel Cl, Southampton SO31	5 F5
Laurel Gdns SO31	5 F5
Laurel Rd SO31	5 F5
Laurus Walk PO13	22 C1
Laverock Lea PO16	15 H2
Laveys La PO15	6 C3
Lavinia Rd PO12	24 A4
Lawn Rd PO13	20 D5
Lawn Dr SO31	11 F1
Lawrence Rd PO15	13 G1
Lawson Cl SO31	4 C1
Laxton Cl SO31	5 F6
Layton Rd PO13	20 C2
Lea Oak Gdns PO15	7 E6
Leabrook SO31	5 F4
Leafy La PO15	6 A3
Leamington Cres PO13	22 B1
Leander Dr PO14	24 C1
Lear Rd PO12	24 B3
Lechlade Gdns PO15	7 F3
Leckford Cl PO16	15 H2
Ledbury Rd PO6	17 E2
Lederle La PO13	14 C6
Lee Rd PO12	24 A2
Leep Cl PO12	25 B6
Lees La PO12	24 B3
Leesland Rd PO12	24 A3
Leicester Ct PO13	23 F2
Leigh Rd PO16	3 B2
Leith Av PO16	16 A2
Lennox Cl PO12	24 C1
Leominster Rd PO6	17 E2
Leonard Rd PO12	24 C1
Lerryn Rd PO13	20 C3
Lesser Horseshoe Way PO17	7 F1
Lester Rd PO12	23 H3
Leventhorpe Ct PO12	24 C4
Leveret Cl PO13	24 C1
Leveson Cl PO12	25 B5
Leviathan Cl PO14	19 F3
Leyland Cl PO12	25 B5
Lichfield Ct PO13	23 F2
Lichfield Dr PO12	24 C2
Lichfield Rd PO14	5 G6
Lime Gro PO16	17 E2
Lincoln Cl PO14	5 G6
Lincoln Ct PO13	23 F2
Lind Rd PO12	25 C7
Lind Way SO31	5 E3
Lindbergh Cl PO13	23 F2
Lindbergh Rise PO15	6 A3
Linden Cl SO31	25 B5
Linden Gro PO13	25 B5
Linden Lea PO16	15 E3
Link Way PO14	19 E5
Linnet Cl PO14	23 H1
Lipazzaner Flds PO15	5 F1
Lister Rd PO6	17 H3
Little Abshot Rd PO14	11 F3
Little Anglesey Rd PO12	25 A6
Little Chilworth PO12	24 A3
Little Cl PO13	20 C1
Little Fox Dr PO15	5 G4
Little Gays PO14	18 C4
Little Green Orch PO12	25 A6
Little Grn PO12	25 A6
Little La PO12	25 A6
Little Park Farm Rd PO15	5 G4
Little Woodham La PO13	23 F2
Littlewood Gdns SO31	4 D6
Liverpool Ct PO13	23 F2
Lock App PO6	16 D5
Lock Vw PO6	16 D4
Locks Heath Park Rd S O31	11 F2
Locks Rd SO31	5 F6
Lockswood Keep SO31	5 E5
Lockswood Rd SO31	4 D6
Lodge Gdns PO12	25 A5
Lodge Rd SO31	5 G6
Lombardy Cl PO13	20 D3
London Ct PO13	23 E1
London Rd PO2	17 H6
Long Dr PO13	20 B4
Long Water Dr PO12	25 C7
Longacres PO14	5 G5
Longdean Cl PO6	16 D2
Longdon Dr PO13	22 C1
Longfield Av PO14	13 F4
Longmynd Dr PO14	13 F3
Longs La PO14	19 E2
Longstaff Gdns PO16	7 H6
Lonsdale Av PO16	16 A5
Lovage Rd PO15	5 H1
Lovatt Gro PO15	13 F1
Lower Bellfield PO14	12 B4
Lower Church Rd PO14	5 G6
Lower Duncan Rd SO31	5 F4
Lower Quay PO16	3 D4
Lower Quay Cl PO16	3 C4
Lower Quay Rd PO16	14 B3
Lower Spinney SO31	10 B4
Lower Swanwick Rd SO31	4 C1
Lowestoft Rd PO6	17 G2
Ludlow Rd PO6	17 E2
Lulworth Rd PO12	22 B2
Lundy Walk PO14	18 D2
Lychgate Grn PO14	13 E6
Lydney Cl PO6	17 F3
Lydney Rd SO31	11 E1
Lyndale SO31	5 G5
Lynden Cl PO14	12 D3
Lyndhurst Rd PO12	24 A4
Lynton Gdns PO16	7 G6
Lysses Ct PO16	3 E2
Lysses Path PO16	3 E2
Mabey Cl PO12	25 C6
Mablethorpe Rd PO6	17 G2
Macaulay Av PO6	16 C2
Madden Cl PO12	23 H4
Maddison Ct PO16	3 E3
Madison Cl PO13	20 D6
Madison Ct PO16	14 B2
Magdalene Way PO14	11 G2
Magennis Cl PO13	20 D6
Magnolia Cl PO14	13 G3
Magpie Cl PO16	15 E3
Magpie La PO13	19 H6
Maidstone Cres PO6	17 G2
Mainsail Dr PO16	14 B4
Maizemore Walk PO13	22 B2
Majoram Way PO15	5 H2
Malcolm Cl SO31	5 G6
Maldon Rd PO6	17 G3
Malin Cl PO14	18 D2
Mallard Gdns PO13	20 B3
Mallory Cres PO16	7 H6
Mallow Cl SO31	4 D6
Malthouse La PO16	3 C3
Malus Cl PO14	13 H4
Malvern Av PO14	13 G4
Malvern Rd PO12	23 H2
Manchester Ct PO13	23 F2
Mancroft Av PO14	18 D4
Manor Ct PO15	5 H5
Manor Way PO13	19 G6
Mansfield Rd PO13	20 B5
Mantle Cl PO13	23 F1
Maple Cl, Fareham PO15	13 E2
Maple Cl, Lee-on-the-Solent PO13	22 C2
Margarita Rd PO15	13 G1
Marigold Cl PO15	13 G1
Marina Gro PO16	15 H5
Marina Keep PO16	15 H5
Marine Par East PO13	22 B2
Marine Par West PO13	19 E6
Mariners Way, Gosport PO12	25 D5
Mariners Way, Southampton SO31	10 A2
Marken Cl SO31	4 D6
Market Quay Shopping Centre PO16	**3 D3**
Marks Rd PO13	19 G3
Marks Tey Rd PO14	13 F3
Marlborough Ct PO12	24 C1
Marlborough Gro PO16	15 H4
Marlborough Rd PO12	23 H1
Marles Cl PO13	20 C6
Marlow Cl PO13	23 F1
Marlow Cl PO15	7 G5
Marsden Rd PO6	17 E3
Martello Cl PO12	23 F4
Martin Av PO14	19 E3
Martin Cl PO13	19 H6
Mary Rose Cl PO15	7 G6
Masefield Av PO6	16 C2
Masten Cres PO13	20 C5
Mayfield Cl PO14	19 F2
Mayfield Rd PO12	25 C5
Mayflower Cl PO14	19 E4
Mayles Corner PO17	7 F1
Mayles La PO17	7 F3
Maylings Farm Rd PO16	7 H6
Maynard Cl PO13	20 C1
Mayridge PO14	5 G6
Mays La PO14	19 E2
Maytree Cl SO31	5 E6
Maytree Gdns PO16	3 A3
Maytree Rd PO16	3 B3
Mead Way PO16	8 A6
Meadcroft Cl SO31	10 B3
Meadow Av SO31	5 F5
Meadow Walk PO13	14 B6
Meadowbank Rd PO15	13 F2
Meadowsweet Way PO6	17 G2
Medina Rd PO14	17 F3
Megson Dr PO13	22 C1
Mellor Cl PO6	17 G3
Melrose Gdns PO12	23 H1
Melville Rd PO12	24 A2
Mendips Rd PO14	13 F3
Mendips Walk PO14	13 F3
Meon Cl PO13	20 B3
Meon Rd PO14	18 A1
Merecroft PO15	6 A6
Merganser Cl PO13	24 B1
Merlin Gdns PO16	15 G2
Merrow Cl PO16	15 G3
Merryfield PO14	5 G5
Merstone Rd PO13	20 B3
Merton Av PO14	16 A5
Merton Cres PO16	16 A5
Metcalfe Av PO14	19 F2
Middle Mead PO14	12 D4
Middle Rd SO31	5 F4
Middlecroft La PO12	23 H2
Middleton Cl PO13	13 G4
Middleton Walk PO14	13 F4
Midfield Cl PO14	13 G4
Midway Rd PO2	17 G6
Midways PO14	19 E4
Military Rd, Fareham PO16	3 F1
Military Rd, Gosport PO12	23 G3
Military Rd, Portsmouth PO3	17 H6
Mill La, Fareham PO15	12 C1
Mill La, Gosport PO12	24 B2

Mill La,
Waterlooville PO7 17 H1
Mill Pond Rd PO12 24 B2
Mill Rd,
Fareham PO16 3 C4
Mill Rd,
Gosport PO12 24 A2
Mill St PO14 12 C3
Miller Dr PO16 3 A1
Milton Gro SO31 11 G2
Milvil Rd PO13 22 A1
Mimosa Cl PO15 6 A6
Minerva Dr PO12 24 C1
Minnitt Rd PO12 24 E4
Minster Cl PO15 13 E1
Mirror Cl SO31 11 E2
Mistletoe Gdns SO31 4 C3
Mitchell Cl PO15 5 H4
Mizen Way PO13 23 F1
Moat Dr PO12 23 F4
Moat Walk PO12 23 F4
Molesworth Rd PO12 25 C5
Mollison Rise PO15 6 A3
Monarch Cl SO31 11 F1
Monckton Rd PO12 25 B7
Monks Hill PO13 19 E6
Monks Way PO14 18 D5
Monroe Cl PO12 23 G4
Montague Cl PO12 24 C1
Monterey Dr SO31 11 E1
Montgomery Rd
PO13 20 C2
Montpelier Cl SO31 5 G6
Montrose Av PO16 16 B2
Montserrat Rd PO13 22 A1
Monument La PO17 9 G4
Moody Rd PO14 18 D4
Moore Gdns PO12 23 H3
Moorland Cl SO31 5 E5
Moraunt Cl PO12 21 H5
Moraunt Dr PO16 15 G5
Moreland Rd PO12 24 B3
Moresby Ct PO16 3 C3
Morgans Dr PO12 19 E1
Morningside Av PO16 16 A2
Morris Cl PO13 20 B1
Morshead Cres PO16 7 H6
Mortimer Rd PO16 17 E2
Mortimore Rd PO12 23 H1
Mound Cl PO12 25 A5
Mount Dr PO15 12 D3
Mount Pleasant Rd
PO12 25 B5
Mountbatten Cl PO13 20 C1
Mountview Av PO16 16 B2
Mousehole Rd PO6 16 C2
Mulberry Av PO14 19 E4
Mulberry Cl PO12 24 B4
Mullion Cl PO6 17 E4
Mumby Rd PO12 24 D3
Murray Cl PO15 13 G1
Mustang Av PO15 5 G2
Myrtle Av PO16 16 A4
Myrtle Cl PO16 20 B3

Newbury Pl SO31 11 E1
Newcastle Ct PO13 23 E1
Newgate La PO14 19 H2
Newgate La Ind Est
PO14 14 A5
Newgate Rd PO14 19 H2
Newlands PO15 13 E2
Newlands Av PO12 24 A4
Newlyn Way PO6 16 D4
Newport Rd PO12 23 H2
Newton Cl PO14 19 E1
Newton Pl PO13 19 G6
Newtown PO16 16 A3
Newtown Rd SO31 10 B4
Nicholas Cres PO15 13 G1
Nicholl Pl PO13 20 C3
Nightingale Cl PO12 23 H1
Nightingale Mews
SO31 5 F6
Nimrod Dr PO13 23 F1
Nine Elms La PO17 8 C5
Niton Cl PO13 20 B3
Nobes Av PO13 20 B2
Nobes Cl PO13 20 C3
Norfolk Rd PO12 21 E6
Norgett Way PO16 15 H5
Norman Cl PO16 16 A5
Norman Rd PO12 24 A3
Normandy Gdns
PO12 23 H3
Norset Rd PO15 13 E1
North Av PO2 17 H6
North Cl PO12 23 H4
North Cross St PO12 24 D4
North Hill PO16 8 A6
North Path PO13 23 E1
North Pk Bsns Centre
PO17 7 F1
North St PO12 24 D4
North Wallington
PO16 7 F4
Northarbour Rd PO6 17 F4
Northarbour Spur
PO6 17 F4
Northcott Cl PO12 23 H4
Northcroft Rd PO12 23 H4
Northern Rd PO6 17 H5
Northfield Pk PO16 15 G2
Northfield Av PO14 13 H4
Northmore Cl SO31 5 F4
Northmore Rd SO31 5 F4
Northway,
Fareham PO15 6 A6
Northway,
Lee-on-the-Solent
PO13 20 B1
Northways PO14 19 F3
Northwood Sq PO13 3 C2
Norton Cl PO17 9 B2
Norton Dr PO16 3 B1
Norton Rd PO17 9 B2
Norwich Cl SO31 4 C5
Norwich Pl PO13 19 G6
Norwich Rd PO6 17 G2
Nottingham Pl PO13 22 A1
Nursery Cl PO13 20 B2
Nursery La PO14 19 E4
Nutash PO14 5 G5
Nyewood Av PO16 16 A2
Nyria Walk PO12 24 D4

Oak Glade PO15 13 G1
Oak Rd PO15 13 E1
Oak St PO12 24 C4
Oakcroft La PO14 13 E6
Oakdene PO13 20 D4
Oakdown Rd PO14 13 H4
Oaklands Gdns PO14 11 G2
Oaklands Way PO14 11 G2
Oakthorn Cl PO13 23 E1
Oakwood Cl SO31 10 C3
Occupation La PO14 14 D1
Ocean Cl PO15 13 F1
Odell Cl PO16 7 H6
Olave Cl PO13 22 B1
Old Bridge House Rd
SO31 4 A1
Old Common SO31 5 F5
Old Common Gdns
SO31 5 F5
Old Farm La PO14 19 E4
Old Garden Cl SO31 11 G1
Old Gosport Rd PO14 3 C4
Old St PO14 18 C4

Old Swanwick La
SO31 4 B2
OldTurnpike PO16 3 D1
Old Wymering La
PO6 17 G3
Oldbury Way PO14 13 E3
Oldenburg PO15 5 G1
Oleander Cl SO31 4 C5
Olive Cres PO16 16 A5
Orangegrove PO13 20 D4
Orchard Cl PO12 21 F5
Orchard Gro PO16 15 G4
Orchard Rd,
Gosport PO12 24 D3
Orchard Rd,
Southampton SO31 11 E1
Ordnance Rd PO12 24 D4
Oriel Dr PO14 11 G2
Orion Av PO12 24 C1
Orion Cl PO14 19 F4
Orkney Rd PO6 17 H2
Orpine Cl PO15 6 B6
Orwell Cl PO12 24 C2
Orwell Cres PO14 11 G1
Osborn Cres PO13 20 A1
Osborn Rd PO16 3 C2
Osborn Rd South
PO16 3 C3
Osborne Rd,
Gosport PO12 24 D3
Osborne Rd,
Lee-on-the-Solent
PO13 22 A1
Osborne Rd,
Southampton SO31 10 B3
Osborne View Rd
PO14 18 B2
Oslands La SO31 4 B2
Osprey Cl PO16 15 E3
Osprey Gdns PO13 22 C1
Otter Cl PO13 23 F2
Oval Gdns PO12 23 H4
Owen Cl PO13 20 B6
Oxford Cl PO16 3 A1
Oxford Rd PO12 23 H2
Oxleys Cl PO14 12 D3
Oyster Quay PO6 17 E4

Paddock Walk PO6 16 C3
Paffard Cl PO13 20 C6
Paget Rd PO12 25 A6
Painswick Cl,
Portsmouth PO6 17 F3
Painswick Cl,
Southampton SO31 4 D3
Pallant Gdns PO16 3 F2
Palmerston Av PO16 3 D2
Palmerston Bsns Pk
PO16 14 A4
Palmerston Dr PO16 14 A4
Palmerston Way
PO12 23 G5
Palmyra Rd PO12 24 A1
Palomio Dr PO15 5 F7
Pamela Av PO6 16 C3
Pannall Rd PO12 24 A1
Paradise La PO14 14 D2
Parham Rd PO12 24 C2
Park App PO17 7 G2
Park Cl PO12 23 H2
Park Farm Av PO15 7 E5
Park Farm Cl PO15 7 F6
Park Glen SO31 5 G5
Park La,
Fareham PO16 3 B1
Park La,
Stubbington PO14 19 E2
Park Rd PO12 25 B5
Park St PO12 24 B3
Park Walk PO15 7 E6
Parker Cl PO12 21 F5
Parklands SO31 5 E5
Parklands PO12 24 B2
Parkway PO15 5 H5
Parr Rd PO6 17 G3
Parry Cl PO16 15 E3
Partridge Cl PO16 16 B3
Passage La SO31 10 A2
Pasteur Rd PO6 17 H3
Patchway Dr PO14 13 E3
Paulsgrove Ind Centre
PO6 17 E3
Paxton Rd PO14 3 A3
Peacock Cl PO14 19 F2
Peak Dr PO14 13 F3

Peak La PO14 13 F6
Peartree Cl PO14 19 E2
Pebmarsh Rd PO6 17 G3
Peckham Cl PO14 11 G1
Peel Rd PO12 24 C3
Pegasus Cl PO13 23 F2
Pegham Ind Est
PO15 6 D3
Pelham Rd PO12 24 B3
Pelican Cl PO15 13 F1
Pembroke Cres PO14 18 C3
Pembury Rd PO14 19 E1
Pendennis Rd PO6 16 C3
Penhale Gdns PO14 11 F2
Penn Way PO12 23 G4
Pennant Pk PO16 8 B6
Pennine Walk PO14 13 G4
Pennine Way PO13 22 D3
Pennington Way
PO15 7 F6
Pennycress SO31 10 D1
Pentland Rise PO16 16 A2
Pepys Cl PO12 25 B7
Percy Rd PO12 24 C4
Pershore Cl SO31 11 F1
Persian Dr PO15 5 F2
Perth Rd PO13 20 C2
Peterborough Ct
PO13 23 F2
Peterborough Rd PO6 17 G2
Peters Cl SO31 4 D6
Peters Rd SO31 4 C6
Petrel Walk PO13 20 A3
Petrie Rd PO13 22 B1
Pettycot Cres PO13 20 A2
Phoenix Way PO13 20 C5
Pier St PO13 22 B2
Pigeon House La
PO17 7 G1
Pilgrims Way PO14 18 D5
Pilning Cl*,
Oldbury Way PO14 13 E3
Pimpernel Cl SO31 10 D1
Pine Trees Cl PO14 13 F3
Pine Walk SO31 5 E4
Pinewood Cl PO6 20 D4
Pinewood Cl PO14 19 F2
Pinks Hill PO16 14 D2
Pinto Cl PO15 5 G2
Pipistrelle Walk PO17 7 F1
Pipit Cl PO12 24 B1
Pitchponds Rd SO31 10 B4
Place House Cl PO15 13 E2
Plover Cl PO14 18 D3
Plymouth Dr PO14 18 C3
Poinsettia Cl PO15 6 B6
Pond Rd SO31 4 D3
Pook La PO17 8 B5
Poplar Dr PO14 13 F3
Poppy Cl SO31 10 D1
Port Way PO6 16 D3
Portal Rd PO12 23 G5
Portchester Heights
PO16 16 A2
Portchester La PO17 14 D2
Portchester Rd PO16 16 A2
Portland Dr PO12 23 F4
Portland St PO16 3 D3
Portobello Gro PO14 16 A2
Portsdown Hill Rd,
Fareham PO17 9 G6
Portsdown Hill Rd,
Portsmouth PO6 17 G1
Portsdown Rd PO6 16 B3
Portsmouth Rd,
Lee-on-the-Solent
PO13 22 B3
Portsmouth Rd,
Portsmouth PO6 17 H5
Portsview Av PO16 16 A3
Portsview Gdns PO16 16 A2
Posbrook La PO14 12 A6
Postern Cl PO16 16 A4
Potters Av PO16 8 A5
Pound Cl PO13 20 C5
Pound Gate Dr PO14 11 G2
Poundbury Cl SO31 5 E3
Poyner Cl PO16 3 C1
Prelate Way PO14 11 H1
Prideaux-Brune Av
PO13 20 C1
Priestfields PO14 11 G1
Primate Rd PO14 5 H6
Primrose Cl PO13 20 B1
Primrose Way SO31 10 D1

Prince Alfred St PO12 25 B5
Prince of Wales Rd
PO12 24 C4
Prinsted Walk PO14 13 E3
Priory Rd,
Fareham PO15 13 E3
Priory Rd,
Gosport PO12 21 G5
Privett Pl PO12 23 G3
Privett Rd,
Fareham PO15 13 E1
Privett Rd,
Gosport PO13 23 E4
Promenade PO13 22 A1
Protea Gdns PO14 12 D3
Puffin Cres PO14 18 D1
Puffin Gdns PO13 20 A3
Pump La PO13 20 B4
Purbeck Dr PO14 13 F4
Purbeck Walk*,
Purbeck Dr PO14 13 F4
Purslane Gdns PO15 6 B6
Pyrford Cl PO12 23 G4
Pytchley Cl PO14 18 C3

Quay Haven SO31 4 B1
Quay La,
Gosport PO12 21 G4
Quay La,
Southampton SO31 4 B2
Quay St PO16 3 D3
Queen Mary Rd
PO16 16 A4
Queens Cl PO13 22 B1
Queens Cres PO14 19 F2
Queens Rd,
Fareham PO16 3 C3
Queens Rd,
Gosport PO12 24 C3
Queens Rd,
Lee-on-the-Solent
PO13 22 B3
Queens Rd,
Southampton SO31 10 B3
Querida Cl SO31 4 B1
Quintrell Av PO16 15 F3

Race Course La PO6 17 E3
Radclyffe Rd PO16 3 E1
Raglan Cl PO13 5 F4
Raley Rd SO31 11 E2
Rambler Dr PO13 23 E1
Rampart Gdns PO3 17 H6
Rampart Row PO12 25 E5
Ramsay Pl PO13 20 C3
Rannoch Cl PO15 7 F6
Ransome Cl PO14 12 D3
Ranvilles La PO14 12 D3
Rapson Cl PO6 17 F2
Rattigan Gdns PO15 5 G1
Raven Cl PO13 23 F2
Ravens Cl PO14 19 F3
Ravenswood PO14 5 G6
Raymond Rd PO6 16 B2
Raynes Rd PO13 22 C3
Rectory Cl,
Fareham PO14 19 E2
Rectory Cl,
Gosport PO12 25 A6
Red Barn La PO15,16 7 F5
Red Oaks Dr PO15 5 G4
Redbarn Av PO16 15 H2
Redhouse Park Gdns
PO12 23 H1
Redlands La PO14 3 A4
Redwood Dr PO15 15 G3
Reeds Pl PO12 24 B3
Reeds Rd PO12 24 B1
Regency Pl PO15 13 F2
Regents Gate SO31 4 C4
Regents Pl PO12 24 D2
Repton Cl PO12 23 G4
Richard Gro PO12 21 F4
Richards Cl SO31 5 F6
Richmond Rd,
Gosport PO12 24 A4
Richmond Rd,
Lee-on-the-Solent
PO13 22 A1
Richmond Rise PO16 15 H2
Ridgeway Cl PO14 16 C2
Ripon Ct PO13 23 F2
River La PO15 7 E3
Riverside Av PO16 3 F1
Riverway Ter SO31 4 C1

30

The Crossway PO16 15 G3
The Crossways PO12 24 B3
The Curve PO13 20 A3
The Dell PO16 14 D2
The Downsway PO15 15 H3
The Drive,
 Fareham PO16 3 A2
The Drive,
 Lee-on-the-Solent
 PO13 20 A3
The Fairway,
 Fareham PO16 15 H3
The Fairway,
 Lee-on-the-Solent
 PO13 20 C4
The Fairway,
 Southampton SO31 10 D2
The Firs PO13 20 D4
The Florins SO31 11 E2
The Gallops PO14 11 H1
The Gannets PO14 18 D3
The Gillies PO16 3 A4
The Glade PO15 7 E5
The Glades SO31 5 E5
The Glebe PO14 19 E4
The Glen PO13 20 D4
The Green SO31 4 C3
The Greendale PO15 7 F6
The Grove PO14 18 D3
The Halliards PO16 14 B4
The Haven,
 Gosport PO12 25 B6
The Haven,
 Southampton SO31 5 G5
The Heights PO16 3 F1
The Hillway PO16 15 H3
The Hoe PO13 20 D4
The Hurdles PO14 11 H1
The iO Centre
PO15 **12 A1**
The Keep PO16 16 A4
The Kingsway PO16 15 H3
The Lane PO12 25 A7
The Leaway PO16 16 A3
The Leisure PO13 20 C2
The Limes PO13 20 D4
The Links PO13 20 B4
The Linnets PO16 15 F3
The Mallards PO16 8 A6
The Maltings PO16 3 F1
The Mead PO13 20 B2
The Meadows PO16 8 B6
The Mews PO12 24 E4
The Moorings PO16 14 B4
The Mount PO13 20 D4
The Nook PO13 20 D4
The Oakes PO14 18 D1
The Old Rd PO6 17 H5
The Paddock,
 Fareham PO14 18 D1
The Paddock,
 Gosport PO12 25 A5
The Parkway PO13 20 A3
The Pastures PO14 5 G5
The Peregrines PO13 15 E3
The Pines PO16 15 F2
The Potteries PO16 8 B6
The Precinct PO12 24 E4
The Queensway
 PO16 15 G3
The Redan PO12 25 C7
The Ridgeway PO16 14 D2
The Rosery PO12 25 B7
The Scimitars PO14 18 D3
The Seagulls PO13 22 C3
The Shrubbery PO16 21 E6
The Slipway PO6 16 D4
The Spinney,
 Fareham PO16 15 E2
The Spinney,
 Lee-on-the-Solent
 PO13 20 C4
The Spur PO12 23 H5
The Square,
 Fareham PO14 12 C3
The Square,
 Gosport PO12 21 H5

The Tanners PO14 11 G3
The Thicket,
 Fareham PO16 15 E2
The Thicket,
 Lee-on-the-Solent
 PO13 20 D4
The Timbers PO15 13 E2
The Vale SO31 11 F1
The Waters PO17 7 G4
Theseus Rd PO13 19 F6
Thetford Rd PO12 21 E6
Third Av PO6 17 H3
Thirlmere Cl PO14 19 E1
Thornbrake Rd PO12 25 C5
Thornbury Cl PO14 13 E3
Thorney Cl PO14 13 E4
Thorngate Way PO12 24 D4
Thorni Av PO15 7 E6
Thornton Av SO31 10 A2
Thornton Rd PO12 21 G5
Thyme Av PO15 5 H1
Tichborne Way PO13 20 D4
Tillingbourn PO14 5 G6
Timor Cl PO15 5 G1
Tintagel Way PO6 17 E4
Tintern Cl PO16 16 C2
Tintern Rd PO12 24 A4
Titchfield By-Pass
 PO14 12 C3
Titchfield Hill PO14 12 C3
Titchfield La PO17 7 E1
Titchfield Park Rd
 PO15 5 H6
Titchfield Rd PO14 12 C4
Tiverton Ct PO16 3 D1
Tollgate Rd SO31 4 B1
Tonnant Cl PO14 19 E4
Topiary Gdns SO31 5 F5
Tor Cl PO16 14 D2
Toronto Pl PO17 24 B3
Torquay Av PO14 21 F6
Tortworth Cl PO14 13 E3
Totland Rd,
 Lee-on-the-Solent
 PO13 20 B3
Totland Rd,
 Portsmouth PO6 17 H4
Tower Cl PO12 23 F4
Trafalgar Ct PO14 13 H4
Trafalgar Sq PO12 24 B3
Trent Walk PO14 15 F3
Trent Way PO13 22 B2
Trevose Cl PO13 20 B4
Trevose Way PO14 11 G2
Triangle La PO14 12 A6
Tribe Rd PO12 24 A3
Trimaran Rd SO31 10 C2
Trinity Cl PO14 24 E4
Trinity Gdns PO16 3 B2
Trinity Grn PO12 24 E4
Trinity St PO16 3 C2
Triumph Cl PO15 13 F1
Truro Cl PO13 23 E2
Truro Rd PO6 16 C3
Tudor Cl,
 Fareham PO16 15 G2
Tudor Cl,
 Lee-on-the-Solent
 PO13 20 D5
Tudor Cres PO6 17 H5
Tudor Ct PO14 13 H4
Tukes Av PO13 20 A1
Tulip Gdns SO31 4 D6
Tunstall Rd PO16 17 G2
Turner Av PO13 20 D5
Turtle Cl PO14 18 D1
Twiggs End Cl SO31 4 D6
Twyford Dr PO13 22 C1
Tynedale Cl PO12 21 E5

Unicorn Rd PO13 19 F6
Union St PO16 3 E3
Uplands Cres PO16 3 C1
Upper Brook Dr SO31 10 D1
Upper Cornaway La
 PO16 15 G2
Upper Old St PO14 18 D2

Upper Spinney SO31 10 B4
Upper St Michaels Gro
 PO14 3 A4
Upper Wharf PO16 3 D4
Usborne Cl PO13 19 H6
Uxbridge Cl SO31 5 E3

Vadne Gdns PO12 24 B2
Vale Gro PO12 24 A2
Valentine Cl PO15 13 E1
Valerian Av PO15 6 B6
Valley Rise SO31 4 D5
Valsheba Dr PO14 18 D4
Vanguard Rd PO12 24 C1
Vanstone Rd PO13 20 C6
Varos Cl PO12 24 A2
Vectis Rd PO12 23 G4
Vectis Way PO6 17 H4
Vengeance Rd PO13 19 F6
Ventnor Rd PO13 20 B2
Ventnor Way PO16 14 D2
Verger Cl PO14 5 H6
Vernon Cl PO12 24 A3
Vernon Rd PO12 24 A3
Veryan PO14 13 G2
Vian Cl PO13 20 B1
Vicarage La PO14 19 E2
Victoria Cl SO31 11 E2
Victoria Mews PO17 7 G2
Victoria Pl PO12 25 B5
Victoria Rd PO12 24 F7
Victoria Sq PO13 22 A1
Victoria St PO12 24 C3
Victory Rd PO14 19 E4
Viking Cl PO14 18 D2
Village Cl PO14 19 E3
Village Rd PO12 23 H5
Vincent Gro PO16 15 E2
Vine Cl SO31 4 C6
Vineside PO13 20 D4
Violet Av PO14 18 D3
Virginia Park Rd
 PO12 23 H2
Vixen Cl PO14 18 D3
Wagtail Way PO16 15 E3
Wakefield Av PO16 7 H6
Wakeford Pl SO31 11 E2
Walford Rd PO6 17 F3
Walker Pl PO13 20 C4
Wallington Ct PO14 13 H5
Wallington Hill PO16 3 E2
Wallington Shore Rd
 PO16 3 E1
Wallington Way PO16 3 D1
Wallisdean Av PO14 13 G3
Walnut Dr PO14 18 D4
Walpole La SO31 4 C1
Walpole Rd PO12 24 D4
Walsingham Cl PO6 17 G2
Waltham Cl PO14 15 H2
Walton Cl PO12 24 A4
Walton Ct PO15 7 F5
Walton Rd PO12 24 A4
Wandesford Pl PO12 21 F4
Warnford Ct PO12 24 A4
Warsash Gro PO13 20 B3
Warsash Rd
 SO31,PO14 10 B2
Warwick Cl PO13 22 D3
Washbrook Rd PO6 17 G3
Watergate PO12 24 E4
Waterloo Rd PO12 25 C7
Watersedge Rd PO6 16 D3
Waterside Gdns PO16 3 F2
Waterside La PO16 16 B5
Watersmeet PO16 14 B4
Wavell Rd PO13 20 C2
Waveney Cl PO14 13 G2
Waverly Path PO12 23 G4
Wayfarer Cl SO31 10 D2
Wayfarers PO13 20 C6
Wayside SO31 4 C1
Wayte St PO6 17 H4
Weald Cl SO31 5 F5
Webb Rd PO16 16 A5
Wedgewood Cl PO14 18 D3
Weevil La PO12 24 D2

Welch Rd PO12 24 A2
Wellington Ct PO12 24 C1
Wellington Gro PO16 15 H4
Wellow Gdns PO14 11 G2
Wellsmoor PO14 11 G1
Wessex Cl PO13 22 C2
Wessex Gdns PO16 15 H4
West Downs Cl PO16 8 A5
West St,
 Fareham PO16 3 A3
West St,
 Potchester PO16 15 G3
West St,
 Southwick PO17 9 A2
West St,
 Titchfield PO14 12 B3
Westborn Rd PO16 3 C2
Westbrook Cl SO31 5 E4
Westbrook Rd PO16 16 A5
Westbury Cl PO6 17 E2
Westbury Path PO16 3 C2
Westbury Rd PO16 3 C3
Westcliff Cl PO13 22 B1
Westcroft Rd PO12 23 H2
Westerham Cl PO6 17 H3
Western Cl PO16 3 A3
Western Rd,
 Fareham PO16 3 C3
Western Rd,
 Portsmouth PO6 17 F4
Western Way,
 Fareham PO16 3 A3
Western Way,
 Gosport PO12 23 G4
Westfield Av PO14 3 A4
Westfield Rd PO12 24 A4
Westgate PO14 19 E4
Westland Gdns PO12 25 A5
Westlands Gro PO16 15 H4
Westley Gro PO14 13 H3
Westminster Gdns
 PO14 5 G6
Westway PO15 6 A6
Westways PO14 19 F3
Weybridge Cl SO31 5 H3
Weyhill Cl PO16 15 H2
Weymouth Av PO14 21 F6
Whaddon Chase
 PO14 18 D3
Wheatcroft Rd PO13 22 B1
Wheatlands PO14 5 G5
Wheeler Cl PO12 24 B2
Whinchat Cl PO15 7 E5
Whippingham Cl
 PO6 17 G4
White Hart La PO16 15 G4
White Hart Rd PO12 25 B5
White Lion Walk
 PO12 24 D3
White Lodge Gdns
 PO16 7 G5
Whitebeam Cl PO14 13 G3
Whitedell La PO17 8 D5
Whitehaven PO16 15 H4
Whiteley La PO15 6 B3
Whiteley Village
Designer Outlet
PO15 **6 A1**
Whiteley Way PO15 5 H3
Whites Pl PO12 24 B3
Whitstable Rd PO6 17 G3
Whittle Av PO15 5 G4
Whitworth Cl PO12 24 A4
Whitworth Rd PO12 24 A4
Wickham Rd PO16,17 3 D1
Wicor Mill La PO16 16 B5
Wicor Path PO16 16 B5
Widgeon Cl PO12 24 B1
Widgeon Ct PO16 15 E3
Widley Ct PO14 13 H6
Wilberforce Rd PO12 25 C7
Wild Ridings PO14 18 D4
Wild Rose Cres SO31 10 C1
Wildern Cl SO31 5 E6
Willersley Cl PO6 17 F2
William Cl PO14 19 E4

William Price Gdns
 PO16 3 C1
Williams Cl PO13 23 F1
Willis Rd PO12 24 D4
Willow Herb Cl SO31 10 C1
Willow Pl PO12 24 B3
Willow Tree Gdns
 PO14 13 F3
Wilmott Cl PO12 23 H3
Wilmott La PO12 23 H2
Wilton Cl PO12 23 H3
Winchcombe Rd PO6 17 E2
Windermere Av PO14 19 E1
Windmill Gro PO16 15 G5
Windsor Rd,
 Fareham PO16 16 A5
Windsor Rd,
 Gosport PO12 24 A4
Wingate Rd PO12 21 E4
Winnards Pk SO31 4 C5
Winnham Dr PO16 15 F2
Winnington PO15 7 F5
Winnington Cl PO15 7 F5
Winterbourne Rd
 PO6 16 C2
Winterhill Rd PO6 16 C2
Wises Alley PO12 24 E4
Witherbed La PO15 6 A4
Withies Rd PO13 20 C5
Withington Cl PO6 16 D2
Woburn Ct PO13 22 B3
Wood Cl PO13 20 C4
Woodbind Walk SO31 11 E1
Woodbourne Cl PO15 13 E2
Woodcot La PO14 19 H3
Woodhall Way PO15 7 G6
Woodlands PO16 3 F2
Woodlands Cl,
 Gosport PO13 23 E1
Woodlands Cl,
 Southampton SO31 4 D3
Woodley Rd PO12 25 C5
Woodpecker Copse
 SO31 5 F6
Woodrush Cres SO31 10 D1
Woodside PO13 14 B6
Woodstock PO14 13 G2
Woodstock Rd PO12 25 C5
Woodthorpe Gdns
 SO31 5 E3
Woodvale PO15 13 E1
Woodward Cl PO12 23 H3
Woofferton Rd PO6 16 D2
Wootton Rd PO13 22 C3
Wootton St PO6 17 H4
Worcester Ct PO13 23 E2
Wordsworth Av PO16 16 B2
Workmans La SO31 10 C5
Worthing Av PO12 21 F5
Wren Way PO16 15 E3
Wright Cl PO15 6 B3
Wych La PO13 20 B1
Wycote Rd PO12 20 B2
Wymering La PO6 17 G3
Wymering Manor Cl
 PO6 17 G3
Wynton Way PO15 7 E6

Yachtsman Cl SO31 4 A1
Yarrow Way SO31 10 D1
Yew Tree Ct SO31 5 F2
Yew Tree Dr PO15 5 G1
Yewside PO13 20 D4
York Cres PO13 22 D4
York Gdns PO16 16 A5
Yorkdale SO31 4 B6
Youngbridge Ct PO16 14 A4

Zetland Rd PO12 24 B3

PLEASE NOTE: No part of this publication may be reproduced, stored in a retrieval system or transmitted in any format or by any means, electronic, mechanical, photocopying, recording or otherwise, without the prior permission of Estate Publications and The Ordnance Survey.

POSTCODES have been reproduced with the permission of The Post Office. Every care has been taken by Estate Publications but The Post Office cannot be held responsible for any errors or omissions. The outward part of the Postcode which is reproduced in this index will not suffice in identifying a particular address. The list of Postcodes is a copyright work of The Post Office.